HOW TO SELL LIKE CRAZY ON FACEBOOK MARKETPLACE

A Guide For Beginners

CHIKA NJOKU

How to sell like crazy
On
Facebook Marketplace

Written by Chika Njoku

Dedication

A big thanks goes to my lovely husband, Charles, and to my lovely kids, Michael, David and Sophie for their huge support, encouragement and understanding. You all made this happen. I love you all.

Contents

Dear Friend,

Your decision to purchase this book "How to sell like crazy on Facebook Marketplace (2024) may turn out to be one of the smartest decisions you have made.

Many of us are on the move to make some extra money, we've either set the plans on how to pay off our debts, phone bill, credit cards bill, or we simply want to make a few extra Money.

But where does the extra money come from?

What do you do when you do not have the time for a second job but need more money to pay the bills? Just think like a boss, take that bold step and try Facebook Marketplace.

If you are looking for a way to make some relatively easy money while also cleaning your house out, you have come to the right place.

In this guidebook, you will learn some ways of making money just by using any of your devices such as Laptops, phones, or tablets. (Be your Own Boss!)

Having used Facebook Marketplace for several years and generated huge income from the platform, I will be showing you some guides on how you can also make money by selling on the platform and be the Boss you are.

In this book, I will be revealing to you the exact step by step process I follow every time I list my items for sale on Facebook Marketplace.

I will also be giving you some top ideas where you can source items you want to list for sales on Facebook Marketplace and how to know what to sell.

Introduction

You have chosen this guidebook because you think it can help you get more money through Facebook Marketplace. You are on the right part as they say, 'no information is too small'. Just think like the boss and act.

I had my Facebook opened in 2008 just for socializing and posting my pictures and making and meeting new friends, just like most people. When Facebook introduced their marketplace, I never understood how and what happens there, so I never gave it a trial.

Fast forward to 2017, One day, I was just playing around with my phone, and I decided to open the Marketplace item to really see what was happening there and I saw so many items listed by so many people for sale, and I saw that It had options for anyone to just add photos straight away without any joining cost, Listing Fee, etc.

So, I decided to look at the top picked items to have an idea on what people really wanted. I did that for so many days just trying to really understand the top pick trends on the Facebook Marketplace.

The next step was to find out where to get the items that I wanted to list for sale.

In this Guidebook I will also be giving you some ideas on how to source for items you want to list for sale.

I was excited to start this new journey on Facebook Marketplace when I got my first product. I made sure I took good quality pictures and followed all the steps I will be sharing with you in this guidebook and went ahead to list my items.

I was so surprised on the huge demands I got that I sold off all items in less than 48 hours. That was so insane!

So, everything I am about to teach you works! You only need to have a device and a Facebook Account, and you can make serious money working from home. So, get ready to be your own Boss!

There are so many ways you can make money on Facebook:

- By being a Social Media influencer
- Affiliate Marketing
- Develop an app
- Selling on Facebook Marketplace.

For the sole purpose of this guidebook, we will be looking at the selling on Facebook Marketplace as one of the ways of making money on Facebook.

Let us dive in!

Chapter 1

Overview of Facebook Marketplace

According to Wikipedia, Meta Platforms, Inc., doing business as Meta, and formerly named Facebook, Inc., and TheFacebook, Inc., is an American multinational technology conglomerate based in Menlo Park, California. The company owns and operates Facebook, Instagram, Threads, and WhatsApp, among other products and services.

Facebook is a social media and networking service owned by Meta Platforms, an American technology conglomerate. Mark Zuckerberg founded Facebook in 2004 with four other Harvard College students and roommates: Eduardo Saverin, Andrew McCollum, Dustin Moskovitz, and Chris Hughes. The name is derived from the Facebook directories that are frequently distributed to American university students. Membership was initially limited to Harvard students before expanding to other North American universities. Since 2006, Facebook has allowed people as young as 13 to register.

Facebook is one of the world's most valuable companies and considered as one of the Big five companies in Information Technology Industry just like Google, Apple, Amazon and Microsoft.

Facebook Marketplace

Facebook Marketplace is the social network's classified ad section dedicated to assisting individuals and businesses in selling items locally. Marketplace refers to Facebook's entry into markets to compete with services such as eBay and Craigslist.

Facebook Marketplace is a platform where users can arrange to buy, sell, and trade items with other people in their area.

It is a convenient destination that connects people to discover, buy and sell items in a safer and more user-friendly platform to use when selling locally.

Anyone can list products or services for sale and gain access to a local audience.

Facebook Marketplace is free but from Jan 2022, Some Market places like UK will Charge a 2% Fee for Postage.

You can sell items on Facebook Marketplace, and the process to list your items only takes a few minutes.

- No setup cost

- No administration fees,

- No joining fee,

- No listing fee, etc.

Facebook itself has 2.8 billion monthly active users with estimated 800 million marketplace users each month.

People tend to think of Facebook Marketplace as a clearing house platform for people to buy and sell their used or unwanted Household items.

By listing on Facebook Marketplace, People can browse listings, search for items for sale in their local area or find products available for shipping.

When Searching for an item on Facebook Marketplace, you can find what you are looking for by filtering results by location, category, and price.

All transactions take place outside of the app and are not considered in any legal sense to be Facebook's responsibility.

One of my best ways of making money from home is by selling on Facebook Marketplace platform. Now, with the new norm of working from home due to the Covid19 Pandemic, this is the best time to turn all those stuffs lying around your home both new and used items into cash.

You can make good money selling good items on Facebook Marketplace.

Whether you are selling, advertising, or marketing on Facebook you need to know how to make money on Facebook using your phone, tablet, laptop, or desktop. Be your own Boss!

Facebook is used by over two billion people worldwide and more than 214 million in the United States alone.

Setting Up Your Facebook Marketplace Account

To have access to Facebook Marketplace, you must have an active Facebook (Meta) account.

Facebook now known as Meta is a website which allows users, to sign up for free socializing profiles to connect with friends, work colleagues, or people they do not know, online. It allows users to share pictures, videos, music and so much more.

Many use it for social networking.

If you already have an active Facebook account, then you have access to Facebook Marketplace. It is located at the left-hand side of your Facebook homepage.

If You still can't see the Facebook Marketplace icon ,Search for it on the Facebook Search Bar

(Type Marketplace).

Facebook Marketplace

Creating a Facebook Account (if not already done)

If you don't have a Facebook account, here are the steps on creating a Facebook Account.

Step 1: Go to   https://www.facebook.com/

It brings you to the landing page as shown in the below screenshot.

Step 2: Click Create New account

It brings you to the landing page as shown in the below screenshot

Step 3: Fill out the quick and easy Form.

Step 4: Click Sign Up.

Note, Facebook account is created for only those over 18 years old.

Now you have a Facebook Account!

Welcome to becoming your own Boss!

CHAPTER 2

Accessing Facebook Marketplace

Facebook Marketplace is available on the Facebook app which you can access with your phones, Laptops, Desktops, Tablets, etc.

On different phones, the Facebook Marketplace icon are located differently.

Example, Samsung phones (Androids) have the Facebook Marketplace icon on the top menu, while iPhones (IOS) have theirs on the lower part of the menu.

To access Facebook Marketplace,

- Log on to your Facebook account.
- Tap on the shop icon at the Top or bottom (depending on the device you are using) of the Facebook app
- and start exploring.

If you are using a laptop to browse on the Facebook website, you can access Facebook Marketplace by clicking the Marketplace icon in the main menu located on the left side of the screen.

Therefore, to start your Boss move, let's go to Facebook Marketplace.

1.To access Facebook Marketplace, click the Marketplace icon from the main menu on the Facebook website or app.

2. If you don't see Marketplace when logged into Facebook, try logging out and back in, or updating the app.

3. Facebook Marketplace is only available to users 18 and older in supported countries

Who can sell on Facebook Marketplace?

- **Anyone can sell on Facebook Marketplace**: Everyone or Anyone who have extra stuff they want to get rid of. Facebook doesn't charge anyone for buying or selling items as at 2021.
- **Business owners**: Start-ups, small business owners, entrepreneurs, etc
- **Ecommerce businesses**
- **Amazon and eBay sellers**

Choosing the Right Items to Sell on Facebook Marketplace

You can sell your personal stuff that you do not need anymore, or you can sell new stuff.

For example, you can sell used or brand-new items like Laptops, phones, television, etc.

If you are just selling out your unwanted stuff, these can also be sold on Facebook marketplace. You can sell large quantities of basic needs that people want.

Facebook Marketplace have some prohibited items they do not approve on their platform.

Make sure you review and adhere to Facebook Commerce Policies before selling your products/items on Facebook Marketplace, these policies will help you understand what items can and cannot be sold on Facebook Marketplace.

Some examples of items that are **not allowed** on Facebook Marketplace include:

- Ingestible supplements

- Alcohol

- Adult products and services

- Real money gambling services

- Digital products or subscriptions

- Ammunition, Weapons, or explosives

- Animals

- Gift Cards

- Prescription, Illegal or recreational drugs

- Tobacco products

- Virtual, Real, or fake currency

- Facebook can reject your item if they feel it is an item on their rejected list. You can submit an appeal and if they do not approve the listing, you just must delete it and try again.

- But most times, they approve the listing once they review and see it is not on their rejected list.

Examples of what you can sell on Facebook Marketplace.

- Earphones

- Smart Watches

- Video Games Consoles

- Women Dresses

- Men Dresses

- Footwear's

- Children Wears

- Phones

Product Research on What to sell On Facebook Marketplace.

You need to do your research to see what people really need/want.

If you want to sell brand new stuff on Facebook Marketplace, one of the ways I do my research to see what people want on Facebook Marketplace is to check the different categories am interested on and see what the '**Todays Pick**' items are.

Today's Pick shows you most of the items that customers are contacting sellers to show interest that they want to purchase the item.

Take note of other seller's product descriptions, price, photos, etc. This will help you when listing your own product. (How can I improve on my own listing to attract potential customers?)

If you are still confused on what product to sell on Facebook marketplace platform, to be the Boss you want to be, you can start from what you have passion for. This will make the sourcing fun for you. Here are some of the best things to sell on Facebook Marketplace.

- Furniture,

- Toys,

- Electronics,

- Phones,

- Clothing

- Tools.

Smaller furniture pieces such as stools, chairs, end tables and shelves do great on Facebook Marketplace because they are easy to transport.

Best-Selling Items on Facebook Marketplace

- **Furniture**: Most People like to sell large Furniture items on Facebook Market place (Example, Beds, Couches, Dining Sets, stools, bookshelves, TV Stands, Mirror, Chairs, side tables,)

    I have personally bought some of the listed Furniture's from Facebook Marketplace.

€70   €75   €155

When listing your furniture, try and describe the condition of the items as much as you can. (Any Scratch or dent should also be mentioned in the listing to keep the listing as honest as possible.)

    Furniture's tend to sell out fast as buyers come with their cars to pick up the items themselves.

- **Clothing, Shoes, & Accessories**: This is one of my favourite categories on Facebook Marketplace.

You can get your brand known by selling on Facebook marketplace.

Make sure you list quality, trending, and affordable wears.

Go with the seasons.

€40   €30   €

- **Vehicles**: Facebook Marketplace is one of Ireland biggest platforms where you can buy New and Used cars.

Potential Car buyers go to Facebook marketplace to search for their dream cars.

€1,999   €39,500

- **Books**: Customers appreciate good bargain on books.

Many college books are also one of best-selling items on Facebook Marketplace.

€8   €25
Business books & dictionaries for sale   IELTS preparation books

- **Seasonal Products**: Listing a product at the right time, sells the product very fast.

Example, Christmas, Halloween, Summertime, etc.

Seasonal Products are very popular on Facebook marketplace and sells out so fast too.

Sold · €20   €123   €123

- **Home Goods**: Home stuffs/ interior decoration unique items sells out very fast too on Facebook Marketplace.

Example, Wall Decoration, Candle holders, Cushions, mirrors, chandeliers, etc

This category is a nice one to go into if you have passion for interior as customers loves unique items at good prices.

€30   €50   €30

- **Garden Tools and Plants/ Outdoor**

This category is very big on Facebook Marketplace. Items sells out so fast in this category

€300   €1,234   €200

- **Sports & Fitness Equipment**.

I love this category too as I sell loads of fitness apparels, etc.

Sports and Fitness are getting so popular, and items sells out so fast.

VAT included

€50   €100

CHAPTER 3

Ideas on how to choose what to sell on Facebook Marketplace

- **What is the trending product now?**

You can see loads of Facebook adverts on any new trending product.

Example, for the female waist trainers, you must have noticed that wrap waist trainer was getting   loads of traffic, that's a good sign on that product.

- **New Product Release**: Always listen out for new product release.PS5 is a big one.

- **Personalised Brand**: You can customise different products and promote.

- **Seasonal Products**: Valentine gifts, Easter, Halloween, Christmas, Winter, Summer etc. Just get creative.

    What will people want during these seasonal times. (Personal Use and gift ideas).

- Everyday Household Needs

Many Sellers always find it difficult to know what to sell on Facebook Marketplace.

The easiest and fastest way to also have an idea on what to sell is by visiting Amazon and eBay sites.

    Check their best sellers' categories and trending deals.

Once you have some ideas, then look around the marketplace to see what other sellers are selling.

Facebook Marketplace Categories

Here is a snip from Facebook Marketplace showing all the various categories.

Categories

🚗 Vehicles

🏢 Property Rentals

👕 Apparel

🏷 Classifieds

📱 Electronics

🎬 Entertainment

❤ Family

🏷 Free Stuff

🌱 Garden & Outdoor

🎨 Hobbies

🏠 Home Goods

🔧 Home Improvement Supplies

🏢 Home Sales

🎸 Musical Instruments

📎 Office Supplies

🐾 Pet Supplies

🏃 Sporting Goods

🎮 Toys & Games

🔄 Buy and sell groups

The Fun part is that you can sell in as many different categories as you want.

CHAPTER 4

How to source for What to sell on Facebook Marketplace

With your Facebook Marketplace research and category research on what product you want to sell, you can start your sourcing process.

Make sure you do your product research on the items you want to sell to be sure it is in demand (So you are solving customer's problems) and it will be profitable to you.

Most important strategy to take on board when sourcing your products are:

1. **Demand:** Are the items you want to sell on Demand? (Do customers want them? If yes, you will be solving a need.)

2. **Competition**: Are you ready to compete with Others? (I always try to sell a bit lower than my competitors. Remember, Customers wants to buy great quality at relatively low price)

3. **Profit**: Will you be able to sell to make profit once you take out all your logistics expenses?

Once all these factors have been considered, then you can start your sourcing process.

• There are plenty online sites that can help you connect with manufacturers of various products around the world. **(Alibaba, etc.).**

So do some online research and be careful of unreliable suppliers and scammers.

• You can also resell products from other retail stores, websites, eBay, Amazon, everything5pounds, etc.

• You can also sell your own customized private label items. (This can be from Alibaba, Aliexpress, Dhgate, etc)

- Find potential Suppliers and attend their event /Trade shows virtually too. It's important you connect with suppliers and ask questions.

Recommended Online sites you can contact manufacturers to buy From

- Alibaba (Very Good Platform for private labelling products)
- Amazon (So many top manufacturers are there, do your research)
- Dhgate
- Aliexpress

Make sure to sample out quality of products before you get your big orders.

How to buy in Bulk for your Facebook Marketplace

Just a bonus for all who wants to buy in bulk or get their private labels. (Go be the Boss!)

One of my best websites where this can help you achieve your goal is the Alibaba Platform.

Here is one of the easiest ways to go about it.

Step 1: Go to https://www.alibaba.com/

Step 2: You can choose the category you have in mind, or you can just type in the search bar for what you are looking for.

Step 3: Go through the different items and make sure you read reviews, check how long the manufacturer has been in business, etc (Do your investigation ..lol)

Step 4: Click on the chat button to talk to them.

Step 5: Try and repeat the process and source as many manufacturers as you can using the above steps.

Step 6: You can buy few items from various Manufacturers just to check quality. (Talk To them about your private labelling too.)

How to sell on Facebook Marketplace

Now that we have found the product to sell on Facebook Marketplace or maybe you have a business with an existing product to sell, I always advice my friends and students to go join as many local Facebook buy and sell groups in their local area before listing their new products.

So, try join as many buy and sell groups within your local area. This gives you a much larger audience.

So many buy and sell groups have huge members in the group already.

Let's go ahead and list our product and start making that money. lol

Step 1: You must have access to a device with internet network. For example, Phone, Tablet, Laptop or Desktop to proceed with product listing.

Step 2: To sell on Facebook Marketplace, make sure you have the items available as customers want them as soon as they indicate interest.

Important reasons why you should Sell on Facebook Marketplace

1.   Large Audience Reach- Sellers tend to reach more potential customers to purchase their brand through Facebook Marketplace.

2.   Great Customer Experience: Facebook Marketplace helps to ensure that your product is been seen by the right audience and therefore increasing visibility and more sales. Therefore, it helps individuals/ businesses to increase opportunity for more sales.

Chapter 5

Process to sell on Facebook Marketplace

Step 1: From your Facebook (Meta) News Feed, click Marketplace in the left menu if using your laptop.

The marketplace icon can be in different locations. Example, Samsung phones (Androids) have the Facebook Marketplace icon on the top menu, while iPhones (IOS) have theirs on the lower part of the menu

Step 2: Click on the 'Create New Listing (If using a laptop)

If using your mobile, just click on the Sell Button.

Step 3: From the Create new listing options, choose listing type.

From the drop-down button, select the option that fits your product.

Example, Items, Vehicles, and House for Sale are my drop-down option.

Let us assume you want to sell a female dress on Facebook Marketplace, you will click the item listing options where it will ask you for the next step.

Step 4: Click the Items Option.

See snip of the landing page you should see once you click on the items option.

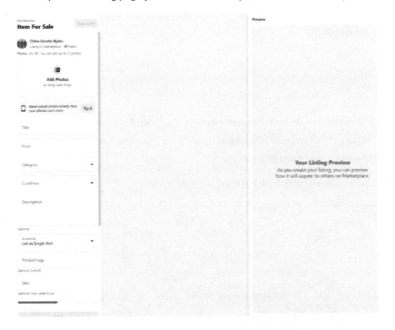

Step 5

•   **Add Photos**: Take high-quality photos for your Facebook Marketplace listing.

(Make sure you take many super quality pictures of your product showing them from diver's angles. You can add as many as 10 Photos of the product.)

One of the best ways to ensure that your item sells quickly is to provide high-quality photos to attract potential buyers and let them see what the item truly looks like. Try taking good pictures with neutral background and minimize distractions so the focus is on the item itself.

Example: When I try to list my clothing items on Facebook Marketplace, I try to show the front view, side view and back view. (Give the buyer all the views they need so they have a better understanding/clarity of the product.)

More Tips on Taking Photos for your products

•   Try taking as many photos as possible of your items by using natural light.

Take advantage of natural light by placing the item in good area with clear lighting, if possible. As an alternative, consider taking photos outdoors in a shady area to avoid harsh shadows.

Also, consider getting the ring lights, tripod stand, photo light equipment's which will making taking pictures easy.

But for starters, just your phone with clear lighting will do the magic too.

Make sure that you're providing an accurate image of the item. If it's damaged in any way, take clear photographs of the affected areas so buyers can see the extent of the damage.

•   Feel free to use an app to brighten and edit the photos. (So many editing apps now available on play store, etc.)

Take your picture to the next level by giving it that professional look. A good-looking picture attracts more buyers.

•   You can get a professional photographer to help you take photos too.

Personally, I do both. (I take most of my pictures with my phone and edit them with my phone apps. Then few times, I get professional photographers to take some photos. These photos are also used for my social media platforms, website, and Facebook marketplace. It's completely acceptable to take photos on your phone for selling on Facebook Marketplace.

•   **Title**: Write a detailed title with keywords in it to describe what you are selling.

This process of listing is where optimization starts from to make sure our products are more likely to sell faster and engaged by customers.

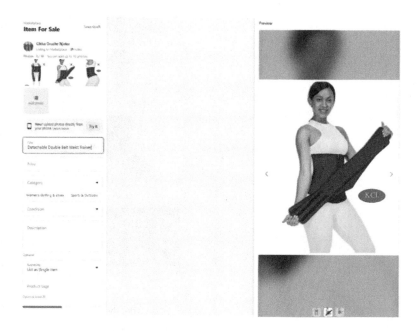

- **Price**: Fixing or setting price for product is a bit difficult. It's important to set a reasonable price to ensure that your item sells in a timely manner. Before setting the price for your product, make sure you have taken on board all expenses incurred /logistics.

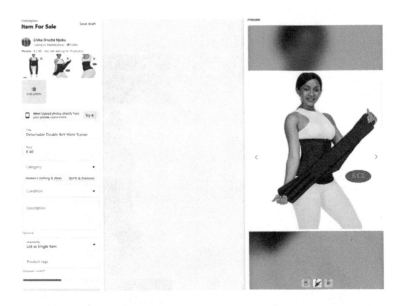

Write the price you want to sell your product. So always consider the right price to attract customers/ buyers. Be willing to negotiate if interested parties offer an amount that's slightly lower than the listed price. It's usually best to be flexible and accept reasonable offers.

Also note that people want to buy great quality and lovely items at a very good, sometimes low price. (My prices are always fixed; I try to sell lower than my competitors. So, this is already discounted.) That's my secret as the best seller in Ireland.

You can include postage cost in your price. This is optional, but make sure to communicate that postage cost is included already in the price.

If you're hoping for a fast/ quick sale, you may choose to fix your price a bit below your competitors' listings.

Also, don't hesitate to set a slightly higher price if you think your item is of better quality than similar products currently listed.

To mark an item as Free, you can enter 0 as the price.

• **Category:** A drop down menu button will show you all the categories available for selection (Baby & Children, Clothing & accessories, etc.)

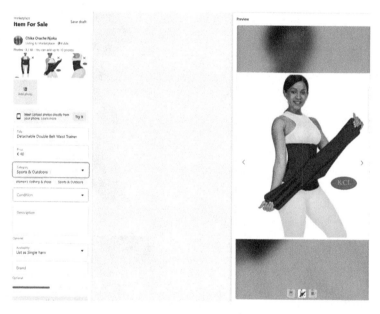

As you create your listing, bear in mind that there are about 30 categories to choose from when you are creating a listing on Marketplace. For Instance, Baby & Kids, Furniture, Tools, Toys & Games, Vehicles, Rentals, etc.

Categorizing your item properly helps customers/buyers to find your product when searched.

So, for example, if you want to sell a female dress on Facebook Marketplace, you will select the 'Clothing and Accessories' category which has 'Women's Clothing & Shoes' as sub-category.

• **Condition**: You need to let your customers know the condition of the product. (Example, if the item is New, Used, etc.) Select the best condition of the item from the drop menu.

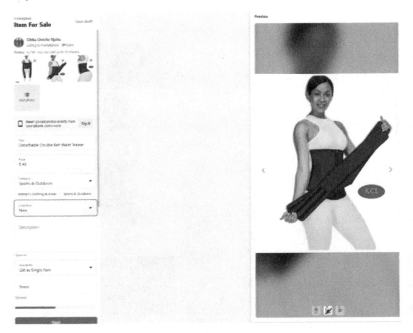

• **Description**: Write a full, honest description of the item you want to sell. For example, Colour and size of the dress you want to sell.

Write as many details as possible about the item you are listing. Include details about the brand, manufacturer, and SKU number(optional). Provide accurate measurements and any relevant details about the item's condition.

The more detailed information your description is and keywords you include the more likely Facebook's algorithm will show your listings to users.

Be honest when describing the item, particularly when it comes to size, place of origin, and condition. You'll only be wasting your own time—as well as the buyer's—if the item doesn't match the description at pickup time. (This could result to negative review which you don't want that for your business.)

Many times, I find so many customers still asking for same information already provided on the description. (It means most of them are not reading it…lol)

But it is the right thing to do (Am sure some customers make out the time to read it.)

So, just write a simple, honest description for the item and make sure that the description matches the product.

- **Availability Function** (New) This was introduced in 2021.

Select the drop-down button and choose any of the options that fits your listing.

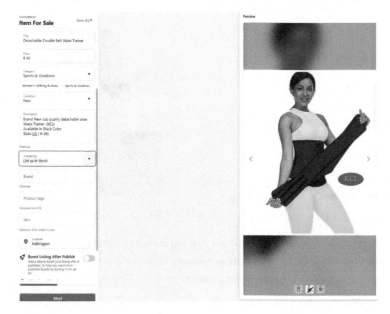

This availability function on Android phone can be found by clicking the additional listing options.

- **Brand:** If you have a brand, this function is one of the best things on Facebook Marketplace. This helps to put the name of your brand out there for more audience to know about it.

   This gives your brand more exposure.

   Good Time to add your brand while listing your item.

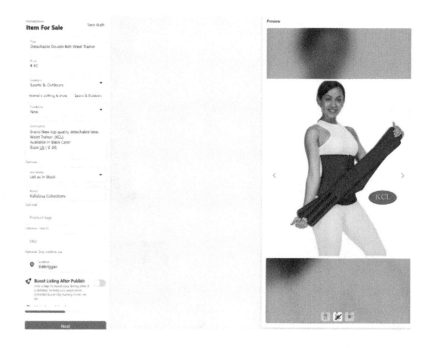

Tags: I love this function and highly recommend you use this in all your listing. Be sure to include search tags.

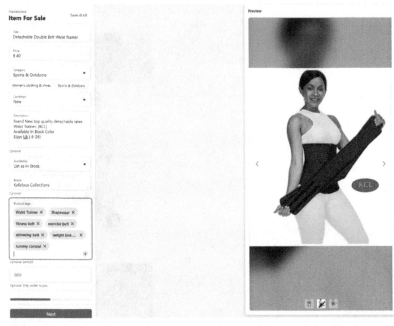

This product tags are one of the best ways customers find your product. First, make sure to list your product in the correct category so it's easy to find.

Facebook Marketplace allows sellers to label their listings with search tags. You can tag as many as you want. The product tags are keywords you think customers put on their search bar when looking for a product.

So, tag as many keywords related to your product. (Up to 20 Tags)

This is optional. But very good to make your listing show up when customers are searching for items in that category.

This product tags helps the Facebook algorithm.

Example, you can tag your product as evening dress, etc. (whatever keywords you feel people will search for on Facebook Marketplace to find it.)

- **SKU**: You can go ahead and write down the SKU for your item.

  (I personally do not use this. I always leave mine blank.)

• **Location**: Your location is also needed so people near you can check out what you are selling, while those far from your location can contact you to discuss/arrange how the item can be dispatched to them.

- **Boost Listing After Publish:** You can turn on/enable the button so that your listing goes automatic to boosting (Paid ADS) Once you publish.

I always leave mine off as I just want to publish without boosting.

Boost Listing is Facebook ads where you pay for your listing to be shown to more users to purchase your items.

Though I have tried the boost options on several occasion, I personally did not see or get any good response.

So, I always turn off the boost while publishing my listing.

Think like the boss, please feel free to try if you want.

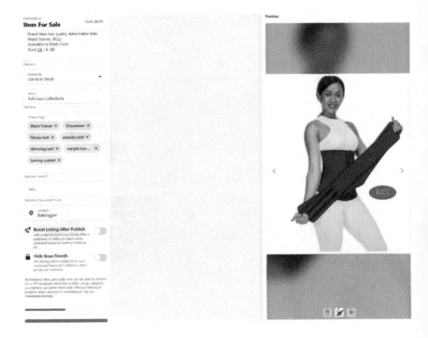

- **Hide From Friends:** You also have the options to turn this function on or off.

Many people are sceptical to sell stuff on Facebook because they are worried about their friends seeing what they are selling.

Feel Free to Turn on the button if you don't want your friends to see the listings.

In my case, I leave it as **off** (I don't mind my friends seeing it. They could be potential customers.)

- **Click Next**: The next button brings you to this landing page as seen below.
- **List in More Places**

  Remember, I asked you to join as many buy and sell groups in your local area. (Once you are approved to join, this groups will show up on the left side of your screen as seen in the snip.

  When listing your item on Marketplace, you have more options to select more places/groups you want your listings to be featured.

  So, scroll down to select as many buy and sell groups you think suits your item.

  I have so many groups with over 150k members.

  Therefore, list your items to as many as 20 groups by selecting the places you want your listings to be featured. (Note, make sure you abide to the group rules before posting.)

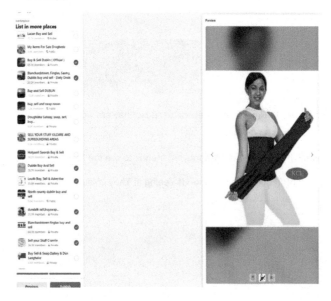

- **Publish**: Once you are happy with your listings, you can now Click the Publish Button!!!!!

44

Click Publish to post your Marketplace listing.

Congratulations, you have just listed your first item on Facebook Marketplace and now we wait for the listing to get approved.

All new listings on Facebook Market place are reviewed by a Facebook Administrator just to make sure it meets the marketplace requirements and conditions of selling. Once the Admin is happy, the product is approved, and you are live, ready for customers to find your product.

Facebook Marketplace review can take between 2 minutes to 2 days for approval depending on the fulfilment of the terms and conditions of selling. But most times, they are reviewed under 5 minutes if no issues are found

Listing Options Differs when using your laptop Verse Phone

When listing using laptop, after the Hide your friend's button, the next prompt button is Next, which takes you to select as many buy and sell groups you want to list your items.

But when listing from your phone, here is a snip of the process

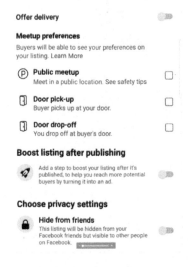

- **Offer Delivery**: You can turn on the delivery option if you can deliver. If you don't want to deliver, leave the button OFF.
- **Meetup Preference**: You can tick any of the meetup preference that suits you.

You can leave them unchecked too if you want.

Choose what's good for you.

CHAPTER 6

How to know when Buyers want your listed Product(s)

Once your product goes live, Customers who are interested in your listing will send you a message which comes up as notification on your Facebook Messenger.

'Is it available'?

This can be customized to the template of words you prefer to use from the settings section. For example, you can change the 'Is it available' template to **'Is this item still available'**? Or use any word(s) that suits you.

Make sure to respond to inquiries quickly.

Facebook Marketplace transactions tend to move quickly, so it's important to monitor your messages closely when you have an item listed. Respond to interested parties as soon as possible to answer questions or negotiate on price. If you don't respond to inquiries within 24 hours, potential buyers may move on to purchase a similar item from another seller.

So, once you get your Facebook Messenger notification of interest from your potential buyer, you both can talk more about the product, agree on the price, payment option and pickup location or postage details.

How To Close a Facebook Marketplace Sale

1. **Respond to inquiries**: Respond to the potential buyer on time. Answer him/her any questions asked about the product (Usually this is done through Facebook Messenger.)
2. **Call To Action**: Find out what they want, give them payment options, collection, delivery, and shipping process option.
3. **Close the sale**: Different buyers wants to know if you can Deliver, or post to them.

So, try and communicate to them clearly on which suits you both.

Be Careful when meeting up with strangers you talked to on the internet when handing off a product

Here are some Important Safety Tips to Note

1.View the Buyers Facebook profile before meeting up so you know what to expect.

2. Meet in a trusted public area where you know there will be lots of other people around. Example, Post Office, Shopping Center, etc.

3. I arrange to meet many of my customers in police stations car park close to my house. This allows both I and the customer a bit of safety feeling. (Because I know the police stations are well-lit and monitored by 24-hour surveillance cameras.)

Advantages of Selling on Facebook Marketplace

1.**Massive Exposure**: Selling on Facebook Marketplace gave my brand a very big exposure.

As of the first quarter of 2020, Facebook boasted over 2.6 billion monthly active users.

So, imagine listing in your different buy and sell groups with over 150k members in different group.

For sellers, new business owners, etc that wants to reach a vast audience or buyers to find their product, Facebook Marketplace is a brilliant platform that will give you that broad audience reach.

2.**Very Cost Effective**: Facebook Marketplace with billions of users has no listing fee, no need to pay for advertisement, etc.

You only need to upload your photos and start selling for free.

From Jan 2022, a postal fee of 2% will be charged to sellers who wants to use Facebook Marketplace postal system.

3.**Instant Communication between you and the buyer**: Marketplace buyers and sellers can message one another through Facebook Messenger.

Messenger chats are fantastic way for business owners to build trusted relationships and make more local connections and network with other business owners.

4.   **Simplifies Buying and Selling:** Facebook Marketplace has made buying and selling so easy. It's so easy to understand and use the platform.

Disadvantage of Selling on Facebook Marketplace

1.   Safety Concerns

2.   Facebook doesn't Vet Buyers and Sellers

3.   Purchases aren't Protected.

CHAPTER 7

How to increase Facebook Marketplace Sales

1.Do some research before you start selling on Marketplace, to see what competition looks like.

This will help give you an idea on how you can introduce or launch your product with good pricing, photos, and description for more sales.

2.Optimize your Facebook listing by including more keywords in the title and description.

3.Use high quality photos: Presentation is everything. You probably won't buy that product if the photo/picture is not looking great, right?

High quality photos can't be over emphasized for your Facebook Marketplace product listing.

The more lovely the pictures are looking, the more they attract the right buyers.

4.Boost: Facebook Marketplace have the boost option which when clicked turns the product to Facebook ad and this brings the items in front of more potential buyers. You may consider using this option too.

What to do if your item isn't selling on the Facebook Marketplace?

Be Realistic and Patient. (Give it Time)

While some items are in high demand and sell quickly on Facebook Marketplace, you may have to wait for the perfect buyer when it comes to some categories.

I remember when I launched a new product, I kept throwing it out on Facebook Marketplace and had no response, kept renewing them whenever they were due for renewal and one day, Boom!!!! (Had loads of notifications, and that changed everything.)

Here are some tips to do if your items are not selling:

1. There may be no demand for what you are selling, So, try and join more buy and sell groups within your area so you can list your items to get more audience.

2. The price may be too high. Consider lowering the price of your listing after a week or two if there's still lack of interest or if the offers you receive are at a significantly lower price.

Customers are always looking out for bargains and will be interested in your items when they feel your price is worth the item value.

If still having low sales or no response, you can consider boosting your listing for a small fee. (This is for those ready to pay for adverts for their listings).

The budget you want to spend on your Facebook boost is totally up to you! You simply enter the total amount you want to spend, and Facebook will spread it evenly across the duration you choose. The average minimum cost of a boost is $1 per day, and that is in your local currency too.

To boost your listing:

- Open the items you listed on Marketplace.

- Click Boost Listing. (Select your Audience)

- Set your total budget.

- Choose how long your ad will run.

- Choose your payment method.

- Preview your boosted listing.

- Click Boost Listing.

But from my experience selling on Facebook Marketplace with highly rated badges, Boosting is a No for me. I have tried it and it did not work for me. However, this does not mean that it does not work.

You can try finding the right items in demand for your buyers to avoid spending money on boosting your listing.

How to Renew Your Listing on Marketplace?

You can renew your listing every week with a maximum of 5 times per item.

To renew your listing on Facebook Marketplace for more visibility, your listing must have been live on the platform for at least 7 days (a week) for the renew button to be active for you to be able to renew your items.

Steps to Renew your Listing:

1.Quick Action Method:

You can renew your listings (Using Phone) by going to your Facebook Marketplace profile (Commerce Profile), then click the quick action button.

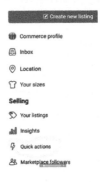

This quick action button opens as the snip shown below

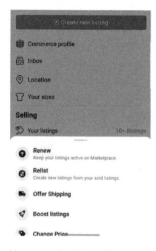

You can select the option you want.

Renew: It populates all your listings due for renewal and you can click individually the ones you want to renew, or you can click Renew all to do a bulk renewal.

Relist: This populates all your items that have been renewed for more than 5 times.

This function is so good. You don't have to relist your items from the scratch, you only need to select the listings you want to relist on to the Facebook Marketplace.

You can do the relist (Delete and relist) individually or you can do a bulk relisting by clicking on the delete and relist all button.

This automatically deletes all the listings shown and they are relisted automatically just like you previously listed them. This new listing can be renewed every week for 5 more times. (You repeat same process again)

2. **Manual Renewal Process**

- Go to your Facebook Marketplace Commerce Profile
- Go to your Listing on Facebook Marketplace
- Select your items you want to renew from your listing
- Click on Manage from the menu on your screen
- Click Renew in Marketplace

How do I edit my listing on Facebook Marketplace?

Here are the steps to follow:

- From your News Feed, Select Marketplace.
- Go to Your Facebook Marketplace Commerce Profile.
- Click on Your Listings.
- Go to the listing you want to edit.
- Select Edit Listing.
- Edit your item's details and then Select Update.

When to Mark your listing as Sold

When a sale has been made, you can mark a listing as sold.

After you mark the listing as sold, it will no longer be visible to anyone else on Marketplace. All buyers/Customers who messaged you about the item will be notified that the item has been marked sold.

Steps on how to mark your listing as sold:

- From your News Feed, Go Facebook Marketplace Commerce Profile.
- Go on to the Listings.
- Select Mark As... on the listing you want to edit.
- Select Mark as Sold.

After you mark the item as sold, the buyer/Purchaser of the item will receive a notification to rate you as a seller.

When to Mark your listing as Pending

You can mark a listing as pending when you have settled to sell the item to a buyer/ Customer, but the sale is not completed yet.

All buyers/ who have messaged you about the listing will get a notification saying that the item is pending. New buyers/Customers will see that the sale is pending before they can message you.

Steps on How to Mark an Item as Pending

*   From your News Feed, go to Marketplace.

*   Go to Your Account.

*   Go to the Listings.

*   Select Mark As... on the listing you want to edit.

*   Select Mark as Pending.

When to Mark your listing as Available

If you marked a listing as sold or pending, you can change it back to available.

Buyers/Customers who messaged you about the listing before will get a message saying that the item is now available. Those Messenger communications will be unarchived if the listing was previously marked as sold.

Steps on How to Mark an item as Available

*   From your News Feed, click Marketplace.

*   Go to Your Account.

- Select the Listing.

- Go to Mark As... on the listing you want to edit.

- Select Mark as Available.

How do I delete my listing on Facebook Marketplace?

Here are the steps on how to delete your Marketplace listing:

- From your News Feed, Select Marketplace in the top left.

- Go to Your Facebook Marketplace Commerce Profile Account.

- Select Your Listings.

- Go to the listing you want to delete.

- Select Delete, then click Delete again.

CHAPTER 8

How to build your Seller Rank on Facebook Marketplace

Buyers and Sellers who have interacted with each other on Facebook Marketplace can rate themselves. So, to build your sellers rank, you need to be:

•   Be active, responsive, and professional: If you can reply to messages about your items within an hour, you can earn the "Very Responsive" badge and your typical response time is listed on your profile

•   Be friendly: Good and excellent communication with your customers at all time

•   Be always completely Honest with your buyers/customers.

•   Punctuality: Be on time with Customers for meet up.

•   Make sure the price is right.

•   Mark your item as sold whenever they are sold.

How to Rate a Seller or Buyer?

On your Facebook messenger chat/ conversation group with your buyers, tap on the customer profile, options of ratings will come up and you can select to rate a buyer

Select a happy face or a sad face.

How to see Your Ratings as a Seller on Marketplace

Go to your commerce profile account and look for the 'Ratings as a Seller' section. You can swipe left to see their Ratings as a Buyer. People can choose to make their ratings as a buyer or seller private.

The rating is a very good tool to have. This helps potential buyers see what people think about your products. (Your rating Stars are visible if you want them visible.)

Types Of Facebook Marketplace Badges

To get Facebook Marketplace Badges, you must have 4 Star or higher rating from at least 4 buyers.

- **Highly Rated Badge**: This means that a seller has been rated positively and consistently by other people on Marketplace. To get the Highly Rated badge, you must have received at least 4 ratings that are equal to or greater than 4/5 stars in the last 30 days. I also have gotten way over 150 highly rated badges from various buy and sell groups.
- **Super Seller Badge**: The Super Seller badge on a commerce profile means that a seller has been posting listings at a high frequency. This badge is only given to sellers in Facebook buy and sell groups.

To get the Super Seller badge, you must have posted at least 10 listings within one Facebook buy and sell group in the last 30 days. I have so many super seller badges, so that's the secret...lol

CHAPTER 9

Top tips for Facebook Marketplace Sellers

• Make sure that your item follows Facebook's Commerce Policies before listing anything for Product/Item sale.

• Never ship an item before you receive full payment. You can request for proof of payment and do your part to validate the proof of payment. Example, the buyer can send you slip of payment for a bank transfer as proof.

• Clearly communicate the shipping timeline, delivery status and tracking information to your buyer. (I always tell my customers that local postage takes 1-3 working days for them to receive goods once payment is received.)

• Consider using a payment option that provides purchase protection, Example PayPal.

• Delivery is another option to sell very fast. If you can get delivery sorted, that will be fantastic. So many Buyers wants the items to be delivered.

How to Report Abusive Buyers

Facebook allows you to report suspicious people or activity on the Marketplace as well.

If something seems off with the customer, stop all communication.

So many Messer can also be found on Facebook Marketplace. These Messer can call you all sorts of names, etc when you are only just on your lane trying to sell your stuff.

What I do when I get such Messer, I just click the report button which I will show you how you can get to the report button.

Once I have reported them, I go ahead to Block users, and this enables them not to see any of my listings in the future

Steps to report a buyer (If using Laptop)

Step 1: Open the Facebook Messenger chat between You and the Customer

Step 2: Choose the More Option Drop Down Button

Step 3: Select the report buyer.

Once the buyer is reported, you can proceed to block the buyer as you don't need the negative energy from that buyer.

Steps to block abusive buyer (If using with laptop)

Step 1: Open the Facebook Messenger chat between You and the Customer

Step 2: Click on the Chat Settings highlighted in yellow.

Step 3: Choose Block a member.

Once the buyer is blocked, he/she can never see any of your Facebook Marketplace listings using that profile.

CHAPTER 10

About Marketplace for Business

Facebook Marketplace for Retail & Ecommerce Businesses

There are many reasons why retailers and ecommerce brands decide to work on Facebook marketplace.

1. It helps them to reach out to more audience.
2. Access to a dedicated storefront for their business.
3. Collaboration with other partners
4. Better Communication with their customers
5. Access to new seller resources such as Selling their products on Facebook Marketplace
6. Order Management Tools such as shipping notifications, onsite checkout, etc.

While Individual can list items for sale, businesses can also use marketplace to:

• Show inventory for retail, rentals, tickets, etc.

• Advertise your store or items on marketplace to reach more people

• Set up a shop with your business page and sell as a business on marketplace

• Businesses can display new or refurbished items from Facebook page shop on marketplace.

Managing Your Inventory on Marketplace as a Business

The idea of managing inventory on another channel might seem like a difficult task when you first think about it, but Facebook Marketplace made it easier.

Before listing your first product on Marketplace as a business, spend some time exploring the following resources about Marketplace policies and best practices:

- Shipping Orders
- Returns and Refunds
- Issues and Disputes
- Adding/Editing Bank Info for Your Shop
- How Sales Tax is Calculated for Your Shop
- State Tax Registration Number for Your Shop
- Purchase Protection for Your Products
- Specifications for Listing Products in Your Shop
- What You Can't Sell on Marketplace

Reviewing these resources will help ensure that you are ready and able to provide the best possible experience to your prospective buyers and customers.

Here are some things to consider when selling on Facebook marketplace as a business

1.   Order Shipment: When selling on Facebook Marketplace, orders must be shipped within 3 days and Customers receive within 7 days.

2.   Not all ecommerce platforms sync with Facebook marketplace.

Here are some ecommerce platforms that are partners with Facebook Marketplace.

- Big Commerce
- Channel Advisor
- Ship Station

- Shopify

- Zentail

- Quipt

- CommerceHub

Big Commerce Merchants: To integrate Facebook Marketplace into your big Commerce store is easy.

Before you get started, make sure you prepare your store for syncing by making sure your stock/product/inventory is up to date and accurate.

From your Big Commerce Store control panel, go to your Channel manager and select Facebook icon,

From there, you will see a box that outlines the rules of marketplace.

Select the box to say you are interested

Once that has been selected, you are all set.

Then we must wait for Facebook Marketplace review process.

This is to allow them review to make sure our products are suitable to sell on marketplace.

Facebook Marketplace Rules

Here is a snip from Facebook about Marketplace rules.

Facebook Marketplace Rules

To learn more about Marketplace, including what kinds of products are allowed and prohibited, view the Facebook Marketplace Commerce Policies.

The Commerce Policies apply to Marketplace, buy and sell groups, page shops, and Instagram Shopping.

1. Certain items cannot be sold.

Facebook maintains a list of items that are not allowed to be sold on Marketplace. These items include:

- Adult products or services.
- Alcohol.
- Animals.
- Digital media and electronic devices.
- Event tickets.
- Gift Cards.
- Healthcare items (thermometers, first-aid kits, etc.).
- Illegal, prescription or recreational drugs.
- Tobacco products or tobacco paraphernalia.
- Unsafe supplements.
- Weapons, ammunition, or explosives.

2. You must sell a physical item.

Anything that isn't a physical product for sale cannot be sold. For example:

- "In search of" posts.
- lost and found posts.
- Jokes.
- News.

Services like housekeeping, as well as event tickets, are only available on the marketplace by coordinating with one of Facebook's partners.

3. The description of the item must match the image.

The photos of the item you upload must match the title and description that you give it.

4. Before-and-after pictures are prohibited.

Items for sale on Facebook can't show a before and after picture (example: a photo showing weight loss).

Facebook has gone through great lengths to ensure that Marketplace is a safe place for people to buy and sell online.

CHAPTER 11

What is the Facebook Algorithm?

The Facebook algorithm decides which posts people see every time they check their Facebook feed, and in what order those posts show up. For its part, Facebook would like to remind us that there is no single algorithm, but rather "multiple layers of machine learning models and rankings," built to predict which posts will be "most valuable and meaningful to an individual over the long term."

In other words, instead of presenting every available Facebook post in chronological order, the Facebook algorithm evaluates every post, scores it, and then arranges it in descending order of interest for each individual user. This process happens every time a user—and there are 2.7 billion of them—refreshes their newsfeed.

While we don't know all the details of how the Facebook algorithm decides what to show people (and what not to show people) we do know that—like all social media recommendation algorithms—one of its goals is to keep people scrolling, so that they see more ads.

The Facebook algorithm isn't static; engineers are constantly tinkering with it.

To make its predictions, the algorithm uses thousands of data points, a.k.a. ranking signals

How Does Facebook Algorithm Work?

1. First, Facebook takes every post available in a user's network (a.k.a. the "inventory"), and it scores those posts according to predetermined ranking signals, like type of post, recency, et cetera.

2. Next, it discards posts that a user is unlikely to engage with, based on that user's past behaviour. It also demotes content that users don't want to see (i.e., clickbait, misinformation, or content that they've indicated they don't like).

3. Then, it runs a "more powerful neural network" over the remaining posts to score them in a personalized way. (For example: Mona is 20% likely to watch tutorial videos from her chess Group, but 95% likely to post a heart reaction to a photo of her sister's new puppy) and ranks them in order of value.

4. And finally, it arranges a nice cross-section of media types and sources so that a user has an interesting variety of posts to scroll through.

So, what does this tell us about which factors get a post to the top of the feed? The answer is that it depends on whose feed we're talking about.

Facebook says that it uses thousands of ranking signals. Everything from the speed of a user's internet connection to whether they prefer to engage by liking or commenting.

How the Facebook algorithm works in 2021

In January 2021, Facebook released new details about its algorithm.

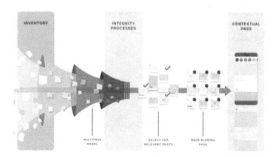

Source: Facebook

In 2024, the platform will still look for authentic accounts posting valuable content and creating genuine engagement. If all your posting is brand promotion, you won't win any bonus points with the algorithm. Instead, focus on creating authentic, informative, and meaningful videos

Facebook Algorithm Ranking Signals in 2021

Relationship
Who a user typically interacts with

Content Type
The type of media in the post (e.g., video, link, image, etc.)

Popularity
How many likes/engagements the post gets

Recency
Newer posts are shown first

Tips for Facebook Algorithm

- Reply to your audience

- Post when your audience is online

- Go Live on Facebook

- Make long video that people want to watch

CHAPTER 12

Facebook Marketplace to start charging some UK Sellers.

Facebook Marketplaces launches a new postal service that allows sellers to directly post items to buyers using Facebook's delivery partner (Hermes) rather than relying on face-to-face collections. Sellers will be charged to use it from January 2022.

Ireland is yet to have this postal service.

Facebook announced that they will start charging Marketplace sellers that chose to send items directly to other consumers instead of handing over the items to them.

This will enable sellers to reach more customers.

This fee will help cover the cost of customer support and purchase protection according to Facebook.

Here are some answers to the frequently asked questions

What Does it Cost?

The 2% charge will come into effect in January,2022 and will be based on the total cost of the item as set by the seller.

In Person Collection and delivery will remain free but from Jan 1, 2022, the 2% fee will be introduced.

Can I Avoid These Fees?

Yes, you can avoid these fees by selecting to list the items locally or face-face collections

Is it available Nationwide?

The new charge will apply to sellers in Scotland, England, and Wales.

What Items can be posted?

Items such as Clothes, Electronics, Toys, Books etc

How will buyers be Charged and Sellers Paid?

Facebook (Meta) has partnered with Stripe a payment platform to process transactions.

Buyers can pay directly through the Facebook Website and are given the option to use their credit card because Buyers don't need a stripe account, Sellers must have one.

Can Buyers Get a refund?

Facebook says all Sales are final. Though buyers can contact sellers to decide for themselves whether refunds can be given when buyers change their mind.

What Happens If there's a problem with Delivery

Facebook says all payments made through Marketplace that meet its delivery eligibility will be covered by its protection policy.

This means buyers can request for refund.

CHAPTER 13

Reasons why you can't access Facebook Marketplace.

If you're unable to access Facebook Marketplace, there are a few potential reasons why:

1. **Location /Region**: If your current location is set to a country that doesn't currently offer Facebook Marketplace, the icon won't appear. Marketplace is available in 50 countries.

2. **Age**: Facebook Marketplace is only available to Facebook users 18 and over.

3. **Account Duration**: If you have a new Facebook account, Marketplace might not immediately be available to you.

4. **Inactive Account Usage**: The icon may disappear If you never or rarely use Facebook Marketplace,

5. **Access revoked**: Facebook could your revoke your access to the service If you've violated Facebook policies when using Marketplace

6. You are using an outdated version of Facebook app.

7. You live or recently travelled in a location where Marketplace is not available.

How to Fix Facebook Marketplace not working?

To fix Facebook Marketplace not working,

Try the following troubleshooting Solutions

Step 1: Log Out and Re login into Facebook

One very simple way to resolve the Facebook Marketplace not working issue is to re-login to the Facebook account. If you are not been able to access the Marketplace, simply sign out from your Facebook account by clicking on the Sign Out button. Wait for a few minutes and login back to your account using your email/phone number and password.

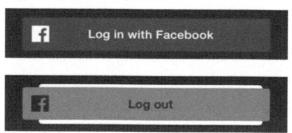

Step 2: Clear Browser Cache and Data: Some browsers prevent you from accessing sites data.

- Log on to your computer,
- Click the three dots on menu on the right corner and click on More tools> clear browsing data

- Set the time range to ALL TIME from the drop -down button

-
- Check the boxes for cookies ad other site data and Caches images and files.

.

Step 3: Update Facebook App

Sometimes, an outdated Facebook app also restricts the users from using the Marketplace. Follow these steps to update your Facebook app and avoid such issues.

1. Open **Google Play Store** on Android or **App Store** on iPhone.
2. Type Facebook in the search bar of Play Store or App Store.
3. As the Facebook app opens, tap on the Update button in Play Store or App Store to install the latest updates. If the app is already updated, the Update button will be replaced by Open as shown in the second image.
4. Wait for some time until the updates are downloaded and installed.

Step 4: Restart your Phone

Facebook Marketplace not working issue can also be fixed by restarting your smartphone. Given below are simple steps to restart android and iPhone.

- For Android users: press the power button on the right side for a few seconds. From three options appearing on the screen, tap on the Restart.

- For iPhone users:
  - On iPhone 12/11/X, press and hold the Volume and the Side button for a few seconds until the phone restarts.
  - On iPhone SE (2nd generation), 8, 7, or 6, press and hold the side button only for a few seconds.

iPhone X/11/12/13   iPhone SE(2nd)/8/7/6

Step 5: Reinstall the Facebook App

Uninstalling and reinstalling the Facebook app can also fix this problem. Here's how to do this on Android and iPhone.

1. Hold your finger on the Facebook app icon for a few seconds until an option box appears.
2. Tap 'Uninstall' and confirm to uninstall the app.
3. Go to **Google Play Store** on Android or **App Store** on iPhone.
4. Search Facebook in the search bar.
5. Click on 'Install' and wait for a while until the app is downloaded and installed.
6. Login to your Facebook account and check if the Marketplace is loading.

Step 6: Change Region/Language

Since Facebook Marketplace is only available in 70 countries, you need to be present in those regions to access this platform. Follow these steps to change your language/region in the Facebook mobile app:

1. Open your Facebook, click on the **Menu**(Android users can find it on the right top, while iOS users can find it at the screen bottom.).
2. Go to **Settings & Privacy**, then click on **Settings**.
3. From the left column, choose **Language & Region**.
4. Click Edit to choose your preferred language.

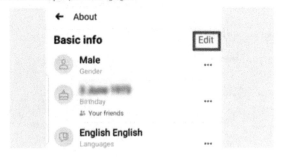

Step 7: Change Account Age

Step 8: Change Internet or Router

If your internet connection is not stable, you might not be able to access Facebook Marketplace. Make sure you have a high-speed internet connection to open the Marketplace and perform your desired activities on it. Hence, try using high-speed internet and connect to a fast and reliable Wi-Fi connection to see if the problem is fixed.

Step 9: Contact Facebook Support.

Facebook Help Center is a 24/7 platform where customers can talk to the company's representatives and resolve their issues online. If all the above-mentioned methods failed to resolve Facebook Marketplace not working issue, report to the Facebook Help Center and fill in complete details about your problem in the form shown on the left. After reviewing your complaint, Facebook will inform you when the issue has been resolved.

CHAPTER 14

Do I need a business license to sell on Facebook?

No, you do not need a business license or tax registration to sell on Facebook Marketplace. You can file for taxes using your social security number. Many people do not like having their social security number hovering around these days so applying for an EIN (Tax ID) number is an alternative.

How to Set Up a Shop Section on Your Facebook Page

•   Look for the 'Add Shop' Section link below your cover photo.

•   Click the 'Add Shop' Section button.

•   Agree to the Merchant Terms and Policies.

•   Enter business details and set up payment processing.

•   The call-to-action button changes to Shop Now.

Please leave a Review if you enjoyed this!

I will be incredibly thankful if you can take 60 seconds of your precious time to write a brief review for me on Amazon, even if it is just few sentences, thank you!

Conclusion

How to use Facebook Marketplace: A Summary step-by-step guide.

Step 1 When you log in to Facebook you should notice a new 'shop' icon Marketplace

Step 2 Click on the Marketplace Icon, then you will be prompted by Facebook to add a photo of the item you are selling. When adding photos, take multiple high-quality photos showing different angles

Step 3 Add a Title to the item you want to list.

Step 4 Add a detailed description of the item you want to list.

Step 5 Set a price for your item.

Step 6 Add your location to let people closer to you find your product.

Step 7 Chose a product Category for your product.

Step 8 Publish your listing.

Step 9 You are Live on Facebook Marketplace ready to start selling (Be your own Boss!!)

Resources

- Facebook Marketplace. (2021). Https://Www.Facebook.Com/Marketplace. https://www.facebook.com/marketplace

- Help Center, F. (2021). Using Facebook. Https://Www.Facebook.Com/Help/1680504982210398. https://www.facebook.com/help/1680504982210398

- How to Make Money with Facebook Marketplace. (2020). Early morning money. https://www.earlymorningmoney.com/how-to-make-money-with-facebook-marketplace/

- W. (2020). Facebook, Inc. Wikipedia. https://en.wikipedia.org/wiki/Facebook,_Inc.

- W.E.B.W.I.S.E. (2021). What is Facebook?

- Https://Www.Webwise.Ie/Parents/Explained-What-Is-Facebook-2/. https://www.webwise.ie/parents/explained-what-is-facebook-2/

- https://www.facebook.com/marketplace/learn-more/business/ecommerce

- https://blog.hootsuite.com/facebook-algorithm/

- https://www.businessinsider.com/how-to-get-facebook-marketplace?r=US&IR=T

- https://www.facebook.com/business/help/289268564912664?id=2427773070767892

- https://adespresso.com/blog/facebook-marketplace/

Made in United States
Orlando, FL
25 January 2025

57819381R10049